Crochet Pattern Collection

Children Jacket´s

By Mandy P.

Imprint

© 2017 by Mandy Puschinski

First Published 2017

Publisher: ThePatternFactory.net, Kelly Dyga, Ballyclancahill, Kilfenora, Co. Clare, Ireland
Email: kelly@micromarco.de

Translated by: Kelly Dyga

ISBN: 9781973190417

Content

CH	Chain	**DC**	Double crochet
slst	Slip stitch	**TCH**	Turn chain
SC	Single crochet	**dec**	decrease
hdc	Half double crochet	**inc**	Increase

Baby Jacket Shell Look Size 62 (3-4 Month)

Preparation

Back and front will be crochet in a shell pattern
Sleeves and hoodie will be crochet in half double crochet
Button line will be crochet in SC
Crochet in hook size 3,00mm US C UK 11
Yarn : Lisa Uni or similar for needle size 3-4 – DK or medium
!!!Each row starts with 1 CH and ends with 1 slst!!!

Materials

Hook size 3,00mm US C UK 11
Sewing needle
5 buttons with a diameter of 2 cm
4x 50g violet
2x 50g purple

Back

Start with violet
63 CH, 62 SC, 1 CH, Skip 1 SC (just this time)
A
*1 SC, skip 2 stitches, 5 DC in 1 stitch, skip 2 stitches *...repeat a total of 10 times – ends with 1 SC, 3 CH, 2 DC in the 1st stitch
B
*1 SC, skip 2 stitches, 5 DC in 1 stitch, skip 2 stitches *... repeat 9 times
→ 1 SC, skip 2 stitches, 3 DC into the last stitch
Now you start over with A.. And over to B.. repeat this pattern over the next (in total) 34 rows
Then you change the colour and cast on for 3 more rows in purple.

Front parts

Start with violet

21 CH, 20 SC, Skip 1 stitch (just this one time)

A

1 SC, skip 2 stitches, 5 DC in 1 stitch, skip 2 stitches

B

3 CH, 2 DC in 1 stitch,

Skip 2 stitches, 1 SC, 5 DC in 1 stitch, skip 2 stitches.... a total of 11 rows

At the end of row 11 crochets 16 CH, Skip 1 CH,

1 SC, skip 2 stitches, 5 DC in 1 stitch, skip 2 stitches

→ crochet now over the already crochet part till the start of the row

→ and crochet another 12 rows

→ change colour after the 12th row and crochet 3 rows in purple

Crochet the 2nd part as the 1st one just crochet instead of 16 CH crochet just 10 CH.

Now place all parts left on left on top of each other. The left part is smaller where the button border will be. Make sure to leave a space of 8 cm for the arm holes when you sew the parts together.

Button border

Spread at the left front part approx. 37 SC evenly. Crochet a total of 5 row of SC.

Button holes

1 SC, 4 CH, Skip 2 SC, 6 SC, 4 CH, Skip 2 SC...... repeat this till the last button hole
→ crochet 2 rows of SC (in each button hole crochet 4 SC)
→ sew the buttons in place and hide all tails

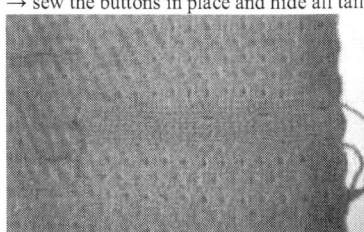 

Sleeves

Spread now over the opening of 8 cm for the arms 35 hdc evenly
Crochet a total of 34 rounds

 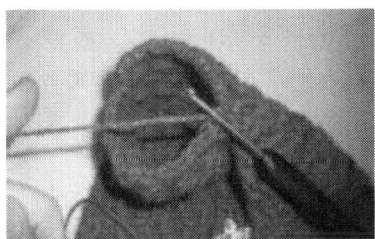

Sleeve band

Dec the 1st with 2nd; 15th with 16th and the 27th with 28th stitch
→ Change of colour
→ crochet 2 rows of shell stitches
Work the 2nd sleeve in the same way.

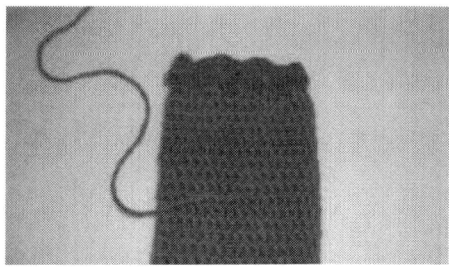

Hoodie

crochet in purple

Cast on at the button border and crochet over the neck line 83 hdc
→ crochet a total of 35 rows
Turn the hoodie over to left side and sew it on the top together.
Now turn it back to right and crochet 1 row of approx. 90 SC in violet.

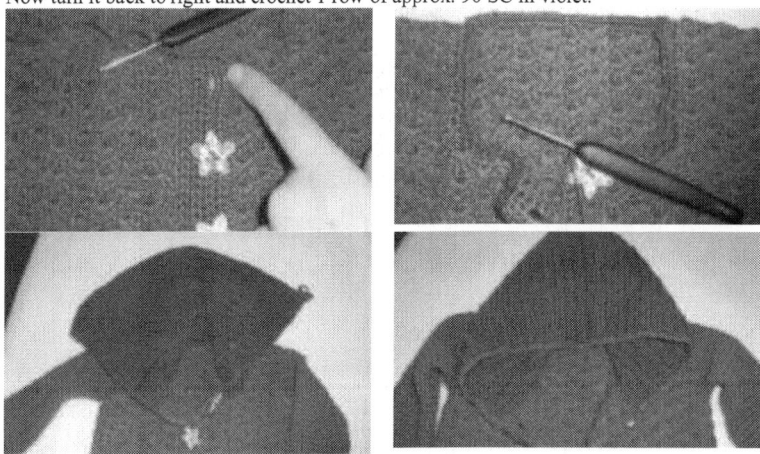

Have lots of fun while you work this pattern.

Baby and Kids Jacket „Woven Shell" – Crochet Pattern

You need

Hook size 3,00 and 4,00mm US C and G UK 11 and 8
Cotton yarn for needle size 3,00-4,00mm (DK or Medium) in 2 different colours
Buttons, Sewing needle and scissor

Preamble

I did think a lot how do I get all the sizes onto paper that you can understand. I hope you are happy with the solution. If you have still some questions feel free to contact me @ kelly@micromarco.de

The jacket

Hook size 4,00mm and crochet from bottom to top
Important that the start CH count is a multiple of 6 + 1!
With hook size 4,00mm this is a guideline:

Size 50/56	78+1 CH
Size 62/68	84+1 CH
Size 74/80	96+1 CH
Size 86/92	108+1 CH
Size 98/104	114+1 CH
Size 110/116	120+1 CH
Size 122/128	132+1 CH

Don't get confused by the pictures. I work the size 62/68 but the work is the same!
As soon you have your chain of CH crochet 1 row of SC.

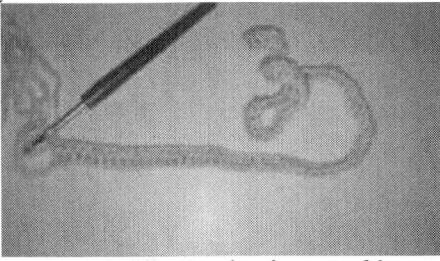

The 1st row of the patter is a little different as the other parts of the pattern:
(below the pictures you find the steps again)

Row 1

3 CH (counts as 1st DC), Skip 3 stitches,
Crochet into the 4th stitch 3 DC, 3 CH,
3 DC into the 2nd stitch of the SC chain

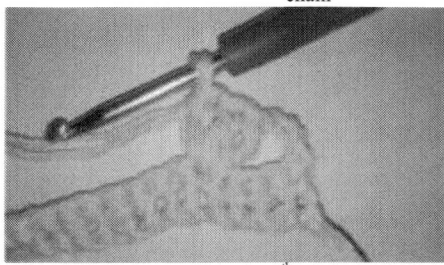

3 CH, skip 3 stitches and into the 4th stitch crochet 3 DC

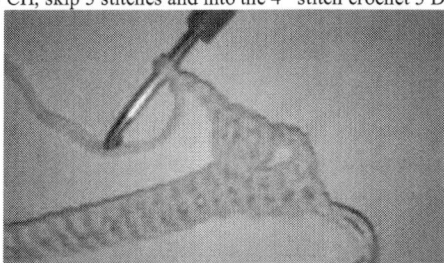

3 CH

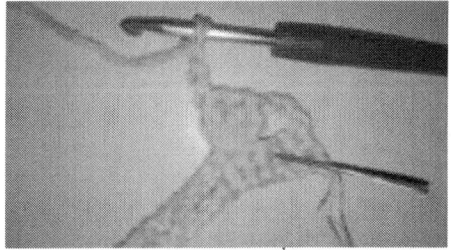

For a better overview I marked the 2nd stitch of the SC-Chain.
Here you crochet again 3 DC in...

now the stitch group is crossing the first time

And ahead...
Skip 1 stitch, 1 DC, Skip 3 stitches, 3 DC into the 4th stitch, 3 CH
And again go in 2 stitches before the 1st 3 DC and crochet again 3 DC

→ now the 2nd stitch group is crossing

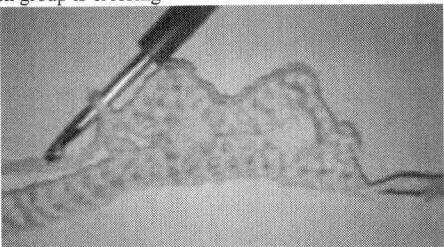

Skip 1 stitch, 1 DC, Skip 3 stitches, 3 DC into the 4th stitch, 3 CH
And again 2 stitches before the 3 DC in and crochet 3 DC
→ now it crosses the 2nd stitch group again
Now you work the row in this pattern to the end!

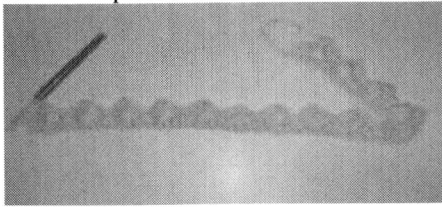

Part A

Row 2   3 CH (counts as 1st DC)
3 DC into the same stitch
1 SC into the top CH of the CH-Bow of the row before
Into the middle DC of the stitch group after the next crochet 3 DC
3 CH
Into the middle DC of the stitch group before crochet 3 DC
1 SC into the top CH of the CH-Bow of the row before

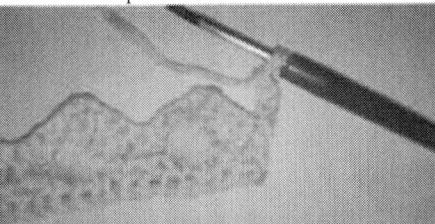

3 CH (counts as 1st DC)

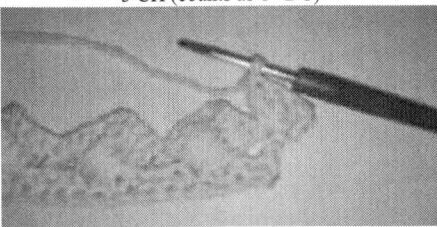

3 DC into the same stitch

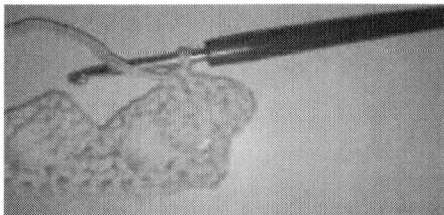

1 SC into the top CH of the CH-Bow of the row before

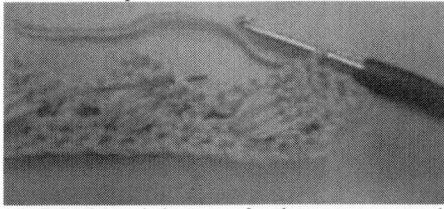

into the middle DC of the stitch group after the next group crochet 3 DC …

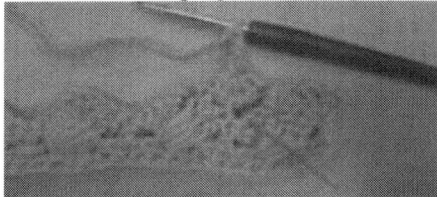

3 DC, 3 CH

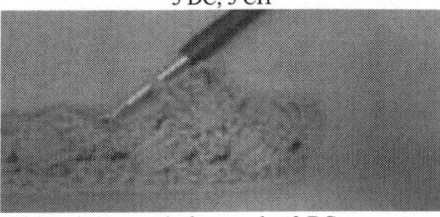

Into the middle DC of the stitch group before crochet 3 DC,
1 SC into the top CH of the CH-Bow of the row before (the hook marks in the picture where it should be)
Repeat this pattern till the end of the row!
Into the middle DC of the stitch group after the next group crochet 3 DC
3 CH
Into the middle DC of the group before crochet 3 DC
1 SC into the top CH of the CH-Bow of the row before
… and so on

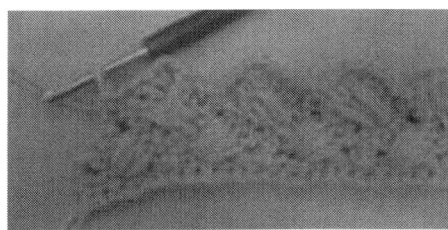

In the last stitch crochet 4 DC.

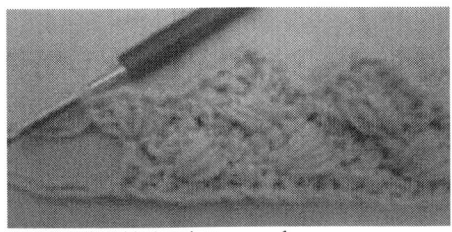

Now crochet the amount as listed below in rows to the top.
A row starts all the time with 1 CH!

Size 50/56	13 Rows
Size 62/68	14 Rows
Size 74/80	15 Rows
Size 86/92	17 Rows
Size 98/104	19 Rows
Size 110/116	21 Rows
Size 122/128	23 Rows

Cut the yarn after the last row!

Shoulders

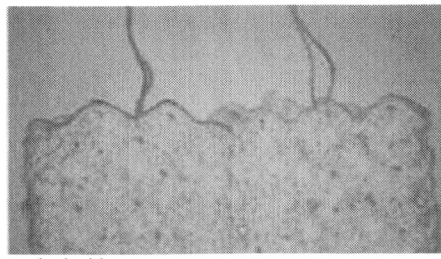

Now fold the sides to the inside.
Place the markers as below:

Size 50/56	6 cm
Size 62/68	6 cm
Size 74/80	6 cm
Size 86/92	9 cm
Size 98/104	9 cm
Size 110/116	12 cm
Size 122/128	12 cm

Place the markers as the table below each to the left or right of the folded parts.

Cast on at the markers and crochet the following amount of rows in the pattern:

Size 50/56	5 Rows
Size 62/68	6 Rows
Size 74/80	7 Rows
Size 86/92	9 Rows
Size 98/104	10 Rows
Size 110/116	11 Rows
Size 122/128	13 Rows

To have it at the right side easier just fold the part open and crochet it on the other side.

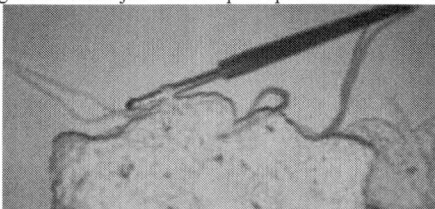
Yarn casted on at the left side.

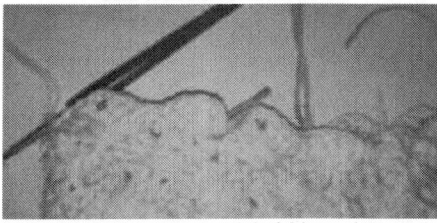

Crochet only till the armpit! That means when it is fold over just crochet it till the armpit (as in the picture)!

If you be that you have to start or end in the middle of the pattern.

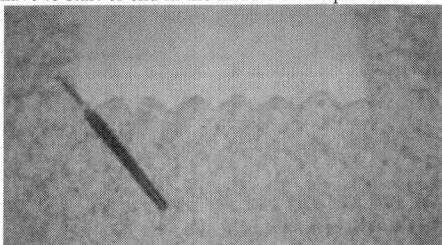
Opened!

Neck

Now we crochet on the here to see inner part.

Cast on the yarn at the side and crochet in the pattern to the other side. It could be that you have to start or end in the middle of the pattern.

You crochet the same amount of rows as you did with the shoulders!

Then you fold the work again over and you sew the shoulder and neck parts together!

With the sewing together you have now the places to place the sleeves!

Hook size 3,00mm - In your 2nd colour

Round 1   Cast on the yarn in the armpit and spread the SC evenly
                 IMPORTANT: the amount of SC must be a multiple of 6!!!
                 Close with 1 slst
Round 2   3 CH (counts as 1st DC), Crochet in each stitch 1 DC, Close the round
                 with 1 slst

Now we crochet the „Relief- Double Crochet "!
This I will explain now in pictures:

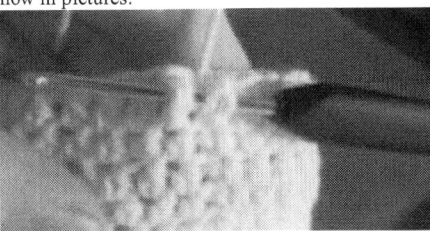

Yarn over as normal
Now go from front to the back once around the 1st DC (as in the picture)
Now you crochet the DC as normal...

And now in the opposite way!.....

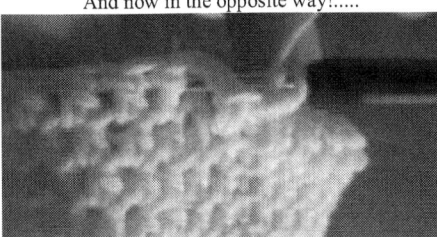

Yarn over as usual around the hook
Now go from back to front and again to the back around the 1st DC (as in the picture)
And now finish it as a normal DC...

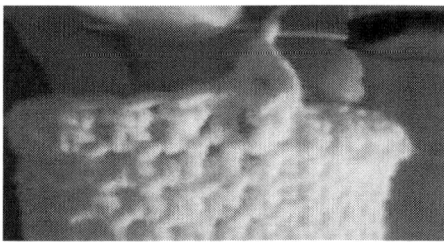

This you do now till the end of the round and close the round with 1 slst!

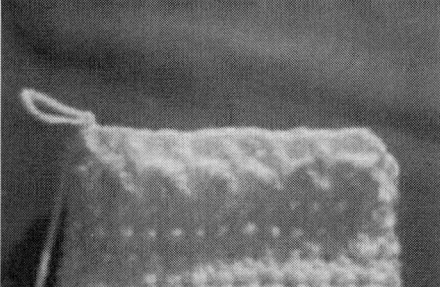

For every round:

Crochet all the time in the opposite way of the DC of the round before. Means is the DC of the round before in the front you crochet from behind.

Is the DC of the round before at the back you crochet from the front!

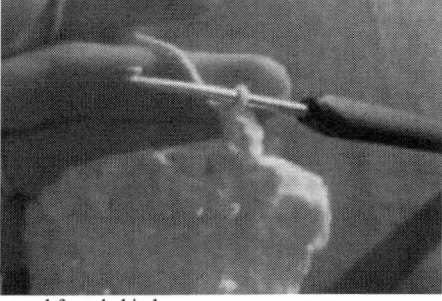

Front DC crochet around from behind

After a few rows you can see the pattern already!

This is the count of rows that you need for each sleeve:

Gr. 50/56	15 Round
Gr. 62/68	20 Round
Gr: 74/80	25 Round
Gr. 86/92	30 Round
Gr. 98/104	35 Round
Gr. 110/116	40 Round
Gr. 122/128	45 Round

Change now back to your 1st colour:

Now crochet 1 more row:

*3 CH (counts as 1st DC), Skip 3 stitches, Into the 4th stitch crochet 3 DC, 3 CH, *3 DC into the 2nd stitch of the SC-chain

→ *repeat till end of round

Here you get the pictures to is: (equals the 1st row of the start of the jacket)

3 CH, skip 3 stitches and into the 4th stitch crochet 3 DC

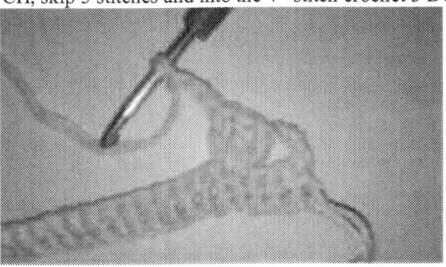

3 CH

for a better view I marked the 2nd stitch of the SC-Chain.
Here you crochet again 3 DC...

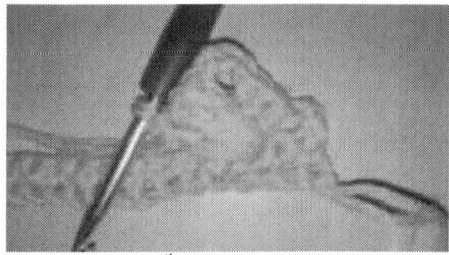

now the 1st stitch group is crossing

And ahead...

Skip 1 stitch, 1 DC, Skip 3 stitches, 3 DC into the 4th stitch, 3 CH
And again 2 stitches before the first 3 DC and crochet 3 DC
→ now the 2nd stitch group is crossing

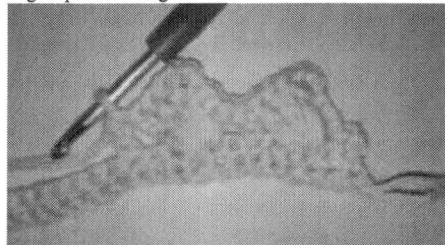

Close again with 1 slst.
Now crochet 1 round of SC!
Cut the yarn and hide the tail.

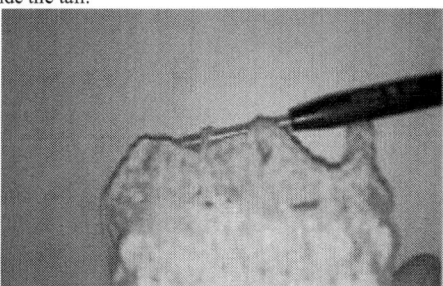

Collar

Hook size 4,00mm - with colour 1

Cast on the yarn at the top left side and spread over the full work SC, it must be a multiple of 6

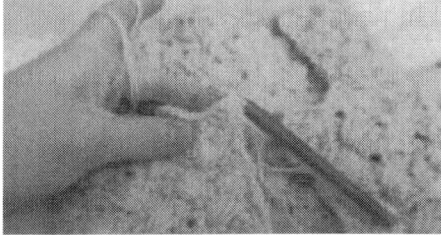

Now crochet 1 row of DC

You start again with 3 CH (counts as 1st DC)
Then you crochet the Relief Double Crochet (DC in a pattern from front and back)
And this as often as mentioned in this table:

Size 50/56	2 Rows
Size 62/68	3 Rows
Size 74/80	4 Rows
Size 86/92	6 Rows
Size 98/104	7 Rows
Size 110/116	8 Rows
Size 122/128	10 Rows

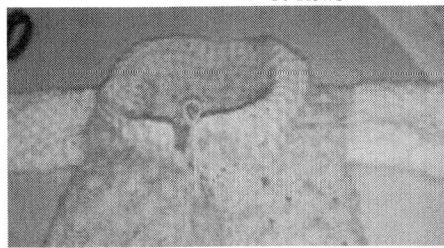

Cut yarn and hide tail!

Button border

Hook size 4,00mm - in the 1st colour
Cast on the yarn in the top right corner.
Spread over evenly SC.

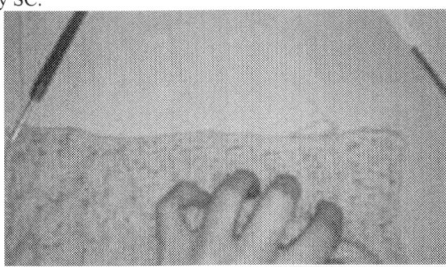

Then you crochet 1 row of DC (1 DC = 3 CH!)
Now Relief- Double Crochet (in a pattern from front and back)
Amount of rows to be crochet:

Size 50/56	2 Rows
Size 62/68	2 Rows
Size 74/80	3 Rows
Size 86/92	5 Rows
Size 98/104	6 Rows
Size 110/116	7 Rows
Size 122/128	9 Rows

Cut yarn and hide tail.

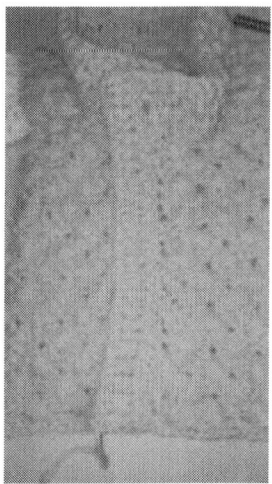

Now sew the buttons to the opposite side in place.

As button holes you use the spaces between the relief-DC.

For the band you just crochet a chain of CH in the length you like. Pull it through the 1st row of the relief DC of the collar.

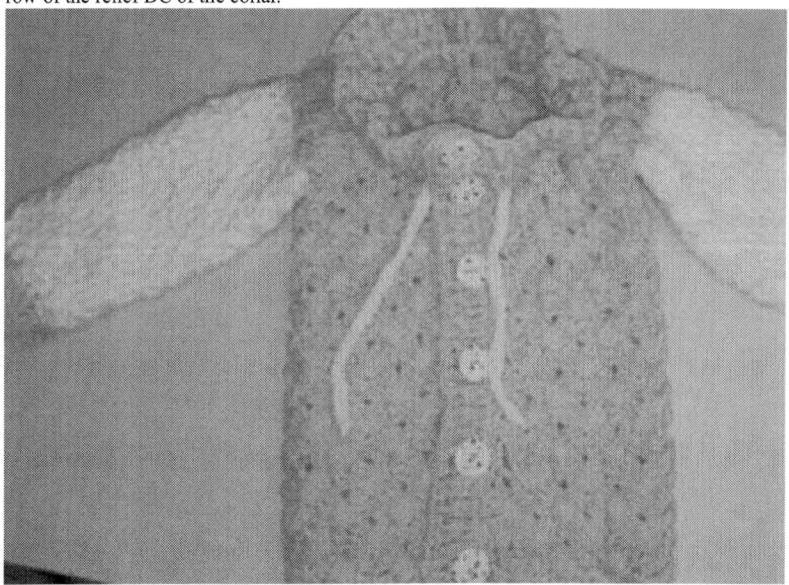

And done is the jacket.

You can of course use the colour mixtures as you like.

Crochet Pattern Kids Jacket with Basket Pattern

You need

Crochet hook 4,00mm US G UK 8
Yarn for needle size 4,00mm in 3 colours (e.g. Sandy Big- ; Omega Color- Lang Yarns -
70m/50 gr equals Aran)
Sewing needle and scissor
4- 5 Buttons
Stitch marker

Front

Make 2

Row 1   22 CH

Row 2   1 CH, 21 SC

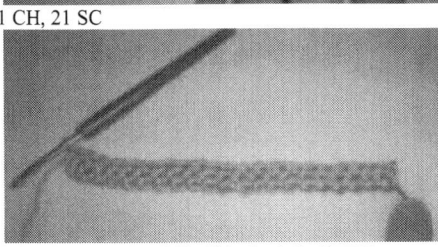

Row 3   3 CH (count as 1st DC), Skip 1 stitch, 20 DC

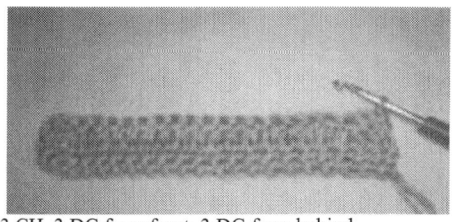

Row 4	3 CH, 3 DC from front, 3 DC from behind
	→ in a pattern till end of row
	3 DC from front:

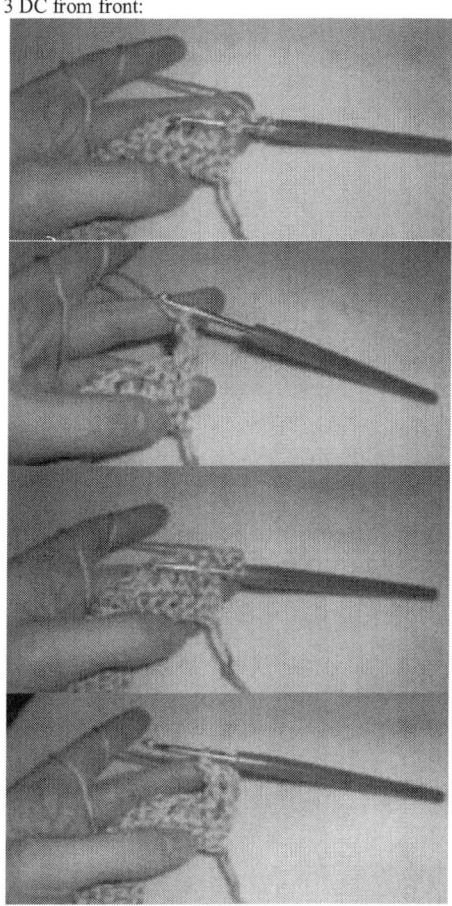

3 DC from behind:

Row 5   3 CH, 3 DC from front, 3 DC from behind
→ in a pattern till end of row

3 DC from front:

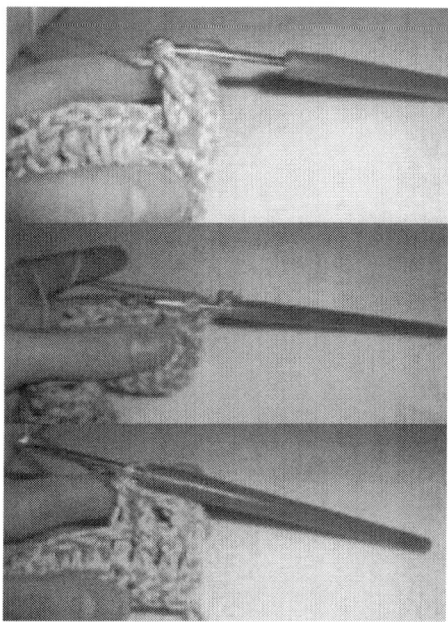

3 DC from behind:

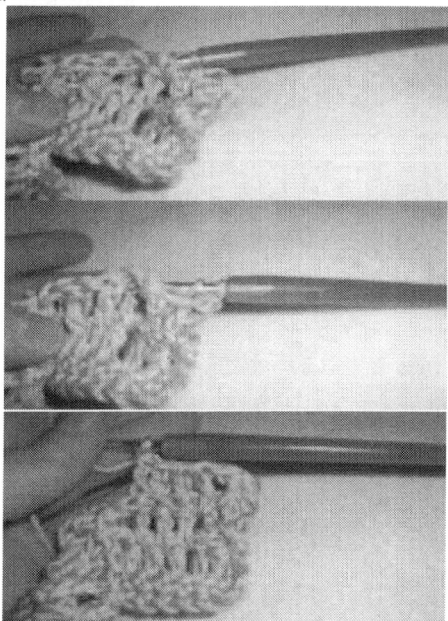

Change of colour

Row 6- Row
7: each

1 CH, 21 SC

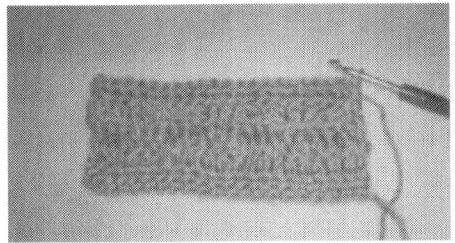

Change of colour

Row 8   3 CH (count as 1st DC), Skip 1 stitch, *2 DC in 1 stitch, 2 DC in 1 stitch, *skip 2 stitches

→ * repeat till end of row. In the last stitch crochet 1 DC

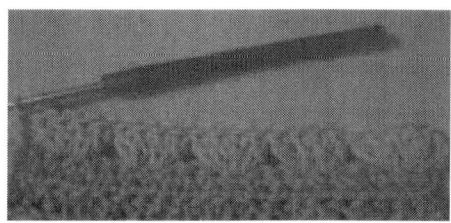

| Row 9- Row 21: each | 3 CH (count as 1 DC), Skip 2 stitches, *2 DC in 1 stitch, 2 DC in 1 stitch, *skip 2 stitches
→ * repeat till end of row. In the last stitch crochet 1 DC |

| Row 22- Row 26: each | As with rows 9- 21
but just crochet into the first 3 stitch groups (see picture) |

Repeat for a 2nd front part.

Row 1	43 CH
Row 2	1 CH, 42 SC
Row 3	3 CH (counts as 1 DC), 41 DC

Row 4	3 CH, 3 DC from front, 3 DC from behind

| Row 5 | → in a pattern till end of row
3 CH, 3 DC from behind, 3 DC from front |

| | → in a pattern till end of row
Change of colour |
| Row 6- Row 7: each | 1 CH, 42 SC |

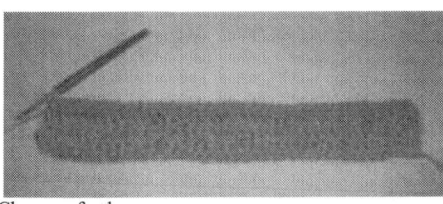

	Change of colour
Row 8	3 CH (count as 1 DC), Skip 1 stitch, *2 DC in 1 stitch, 2 DC in 1 stitch, *skip 2 stitches
→	*repeat till end of row. Into the last stitch 1 DC.

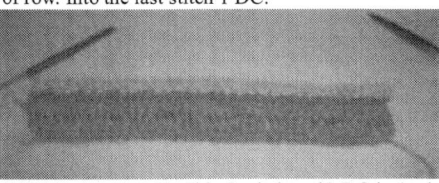

| Row 9- Row 26: each | 3 CH (count as 1 DC), Skip 2 stitches, *2 DC in 1 stitch, 2 DC in 1 stitch, *skip 2 stitches |
| → | *repeat till end of row. Into the last stitch crochet 1 DC. |

Now sew the shoulders together.
Sew also the sides together. For this count at the front and back part 7 rows from top.
Place a marker between row 7 and 8. Then you start to sew the parts from bottom to top together till you reach the markers. Then fasten off and hide the tail.
Turn the work back to right.

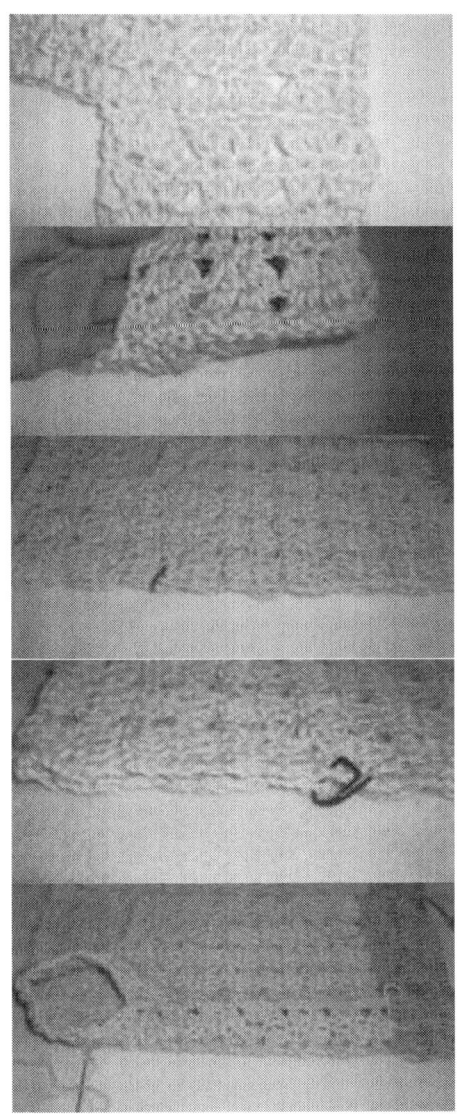

Sleeves

Round 1   Cast on the axle and crochet evenly spread 32 hdc

Round 2   3 CH (counts as 1st DC), Skip 1 stitch, *2 DC in 1 stitch, 2 DC in 1 stitch, *skip 2 stitches

→ *repeat till end of round. Into the last stitch crochet 1 DC. Finish the round with 1 slst.

Round 3-   3 LM (counts as 1st DC), Skip 2 stitches, *2 DC in 1 stitch, 2 DC in 1
Round 10: each   stitch, *skip 2 stitches

→ *repeat till end of round. Into the last stitch crochet 1 DC. Finish the round with 1 slst

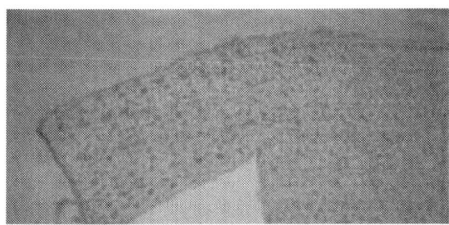

Change of colour
Round 11-   1 CH, 33 hdc, 1 slst
Round 14: each

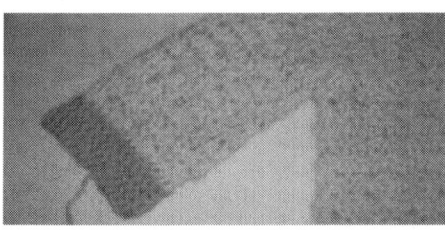

Change of colour
Round 15   3 CH (counts as 1st DC), Skip 1 stitch, 32 DC, 1 slst

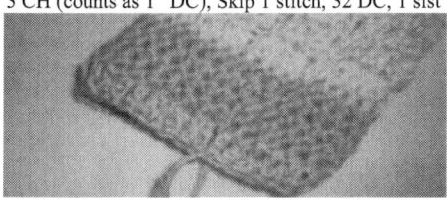

Round 16   3 CH, 3 DC relief from front, 3 DC relief from behind
→ in a pattern till end of the round, finish the round with 1 slst
Round 17   3 CH, 3 DC relief from behind, 3 DC relief from front
→ in a pattern till end of the round, finish the round with 1 slst

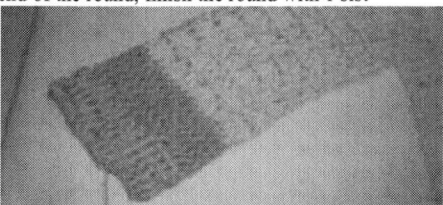

Crochet the 2nd sleeve in the same way:

Right button border
Row 1   Cast on at the top and spread 2 hdc evenly

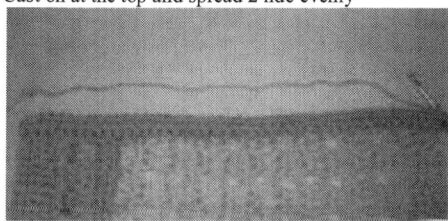

| Row 2 | 1 CH, 2 hdc, 2 CH, Skip 1 stitch (1st button hole), 11 hdc, 2 CH, Skip 1 stitch (2nd button hole), 11 hdc, 2 CH, Skip 1 stitch (3rd button hole), 11 hdc, 2 CH, Skip 1 stitch (4th button hole), 4 hdc |

Row 2   1 CH, 2 hdc, 2 CH, Skip 1 stitch (1st button hole), 11 hdc, 2 CH, Skip 1 stitch (2nd button hole), 11 hdc, 2 CH, Skip 1 stitch (3rd button hole), 11 hdc, 2 CH, Skip 1 stitch (4th button hole), 4 hdc

Row 3   In each stitch 1 hdc, In each chain bow 2 hdc

Sew the buttons to the other side.
Now you need to decide if you like a collar or a hoodie. Both will be explained below

Collar

Row 1   Cast on at the top left and crochet around the neck line back down = 62 hdc

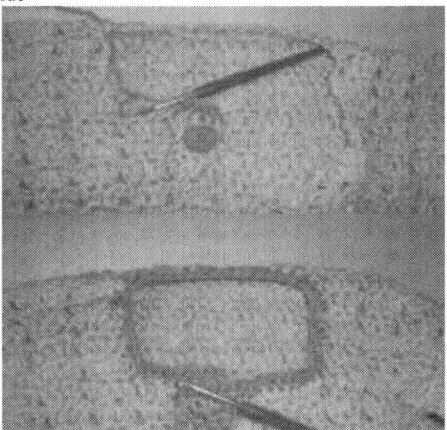

Row 2   3 CH (counts as 1st DC), Skip 1 stitch, *2 DC into 1 stitch, 2 DC into 1 stitch, *skip 2 stitches
→ * repeat till end of row. Into the last stitch crochet 1 DC.

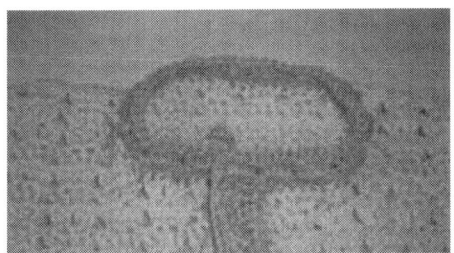

Row 3- Row 5   3 CH (counts as 1st DC), Skip 2 stitches, *2 DC in 1 stitch, 2 DC in 1 stitch, *skip 2 stitches
→ * repeat till end of row. Into the last stitch crochet 1 DC

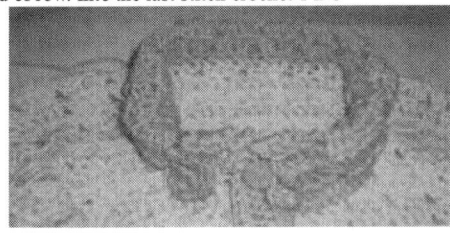

Hoodie

Row 1   Cast on at the top left corner and crochet (over the back) to the other side = 62 hdc

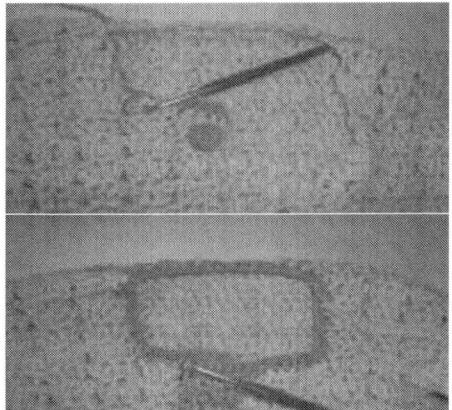

Row 2   3 CH (counts as 1st DC), Skip 1 stitch, *2 DC in 1 stitch, 2 DC in 1 stitch, *skip 2 stitches
→ * repeat till end of row. Into the last stitch crochet 1 DC.

Row 3- Row 17   3 CH (counts as 1st DC), Skip 2 stitches, *2 DC in 1 stitch, 2 DC in 1 stitch, *skip 2 stitches
→ * repeat till end of row. Into the last stitch crochet 1 DC.

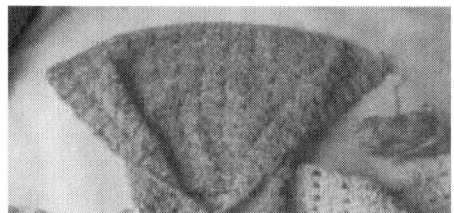

Change of colour
Row 18   1 CH, 60 hdc

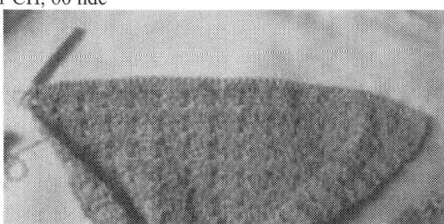

Row 19   3 CH (counts as 1st DC), Skip 1 stitch, 59 DC

Row 20   3 CH, 3 DC from front, 3 DC from behind

→ repeat in a pattern till end of row
Fold the hoodie to the left and sew it on top together.

Hide all tails.

And done is the jacket :-)

Children Jacket – Crochet Pattern

Size Table

Age	Size	Bust	Waist	
2-3Y	90-98 cm	52-54 cm	48-50 cm	
3-4Y	98-104 cm	54-56 cm	50-52 cm	
4-5Y	104-110 cm	56-58 cm	52-53.5 cm	
5-6Y	110-116 cm	58-60 cm	53.5-55 cm	
6-7Y	116-122 cm	60-62 cm	55-56.5 cm	
7-8Y	122-128 cm	62-64 cm	56.5-58 cm	

Age	Size	Bust	Waist
0-3m	till 60 cm	till 42 cm	till 39 cm
3-6m	60-68 cm	42-46 cm	39-43 cm
6-12m	68-76 cm	46-48 cm	43-44 cm
12-18m	76-83 cm	48-50 cm	44-46 cm
18-24m	83-90 cm	50-52 cm	46-48 cm

Needed Materials

Hook sizes 5,00mm 8,00mm and 10,00mm US H, N UK 6, 0, 000
8x 50 Gramm Yarn "Wolke Hegenbarth ,, Urban Roots'" 60m/50gr equal Chunky
1x 50 Gramm Yarn "Indian Summer" equals 50m/50 gr – bulky yarn
→ or similar yarn for hook size 8-10
Sewing needle, Measuring tape
7 buttons in a diameter of approx. 2cm

Measurements

This jacket you can crochet easily in all sizes. You just need the following measurements:

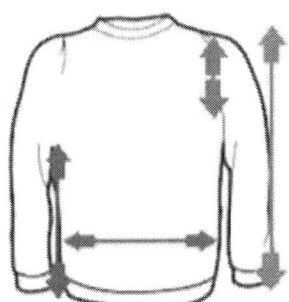

Height of jacket
Circumference
Sleeve circumference
Sleeve length

I work in this sample size DEU 122 for children
(Height of jacket 40 cm
Circumference 60 cm
Sleeve circumference 24 cm → you need the half of the height of the shoulder – means 12
cm Sleeve length 40 cm)
We start at the main part at the shoulders. The shoulder and the neck/collar will be later
crochet in place. The same with the sleeve and the button border.
The pictures will assist you to understand the pattern if you crochet it in a different size.
And now have lots of fun :)

Main Part
Hook size 10,00mm

Each row starts with a TCH
63 CH
Go into the 2nd CH from hook and crochet 61 SC
Now crochet in a pattern 1 SC and 1 CH. Skip with the CH 1 SC

→ so you get the tweed pattern
Crochet another 42 rows in this pattern

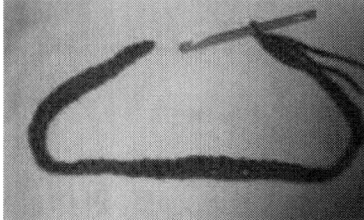 

Fold the sides together and leave approx. 6cm space in between

Now count the stitches on the top border that will form the shoulders.
Count ONLY the SC of the row before.
Cast the yarn on 3 SC away from the neck line and start crocheting in the 4th SC.
From here you work 10 rows of each 6 SC (in tweed pattern)
Cut the yarn and crochet the 2nd shoulder in the same way.

 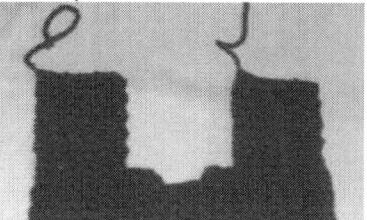

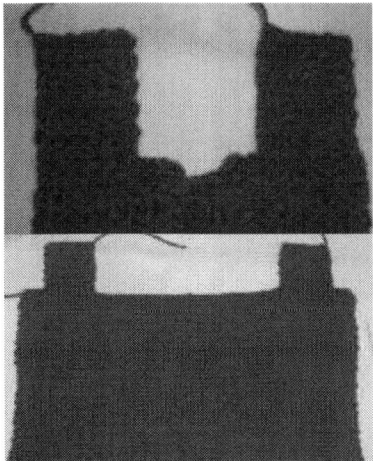

Fold the work open.
Leave 1 SC space and crochet to the 2nd shoulder part. Also here stop 1 SC before the shoulder part ends. Repeat this in a total of 10 rows.
Remember: crochet only into the SC of the row before and ignore the CH!

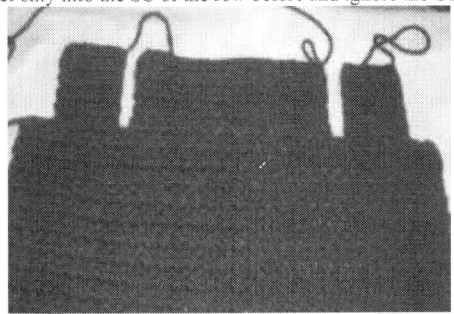

Now fold the work over to the left and sew the shoulder parts at the top together. Leave the sides open. Later you will start here with the sleeves. Then turn the work back to normal.

Sleeves

Hook size 8,00mm; crochet the sleeves in hdc
Each round starts with a slst and ends with a CH
Start at the right sleeve and spread evenly approx. 24 hdc over the opening
You crochet all together 30 rounds

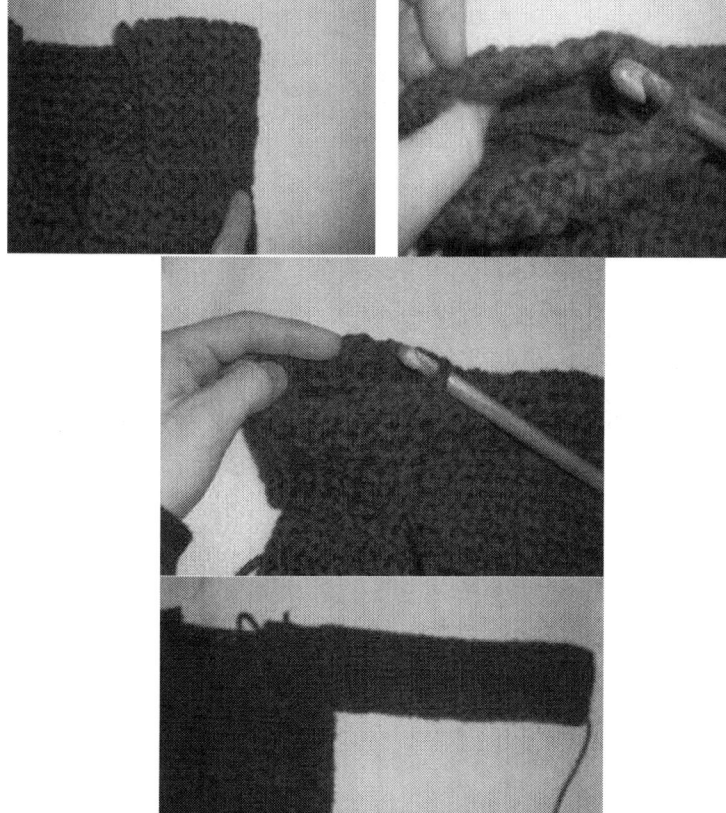

Start the left sleeve at the top of the shoulder. Spread again 24 hdc over the opening and crochet 30 rounds.

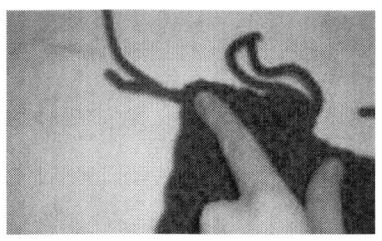

Hook size 8,00 mm
Each row starts with 1 CH
Start at the left bottom
Spread approx. 128 hdc from left over the neck line down to the right
Crochet once back to where you started
!!!At the neckline you crochet 2x 2 hdc in 1 stitch!!!
The collar will lift up now
And now crochet again back to the right bottom

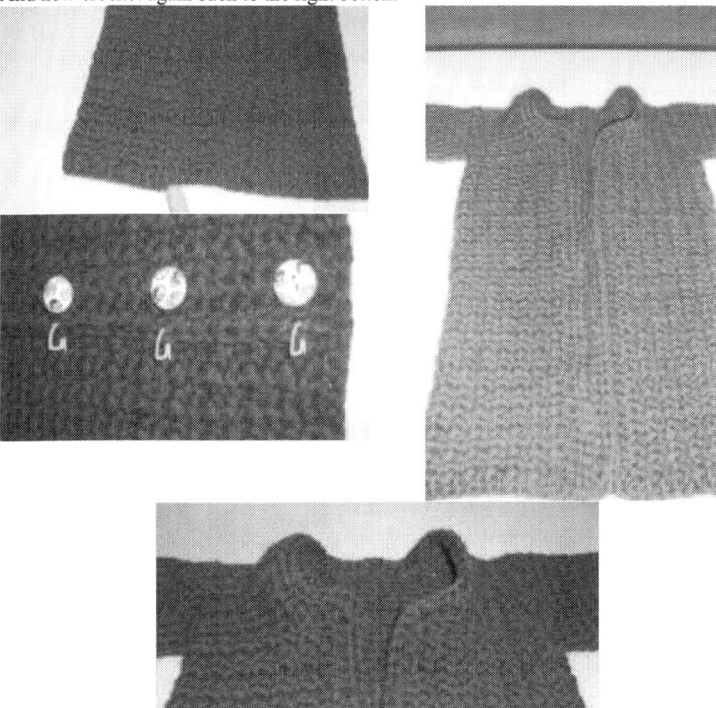

At the neck line crochet 2x 2hdc in 1 stitch

Now place the buttons to where you like to place them. Mark them with stitch markers. Now you start again with hdc. Where you have the marker placed you just skip the SC and crochet an CH instead. Crochet all over to the other side.

Now crochet again back. Into the CH of the row before you crochet each 1 hdc and finish the row at the button border on the right bottom side

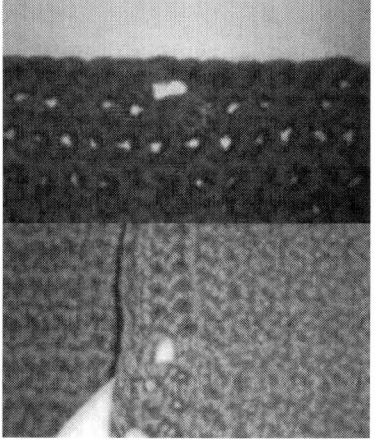

Now place the sides over. The button border is on top. Make sure everything is straight and on top of each other.

Place a marker through the button hole onto the other side.

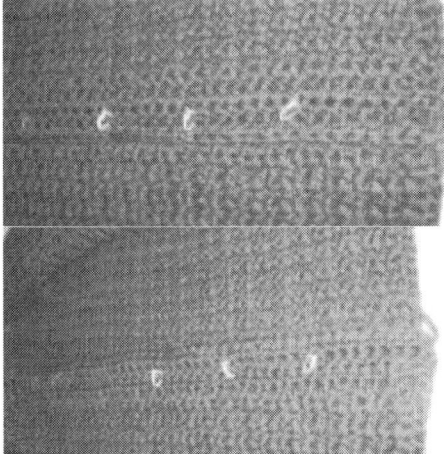

Open the work again and sew the buttons to the marked places.

Hook size 5,00mm

15 CH

Into the 2nd CH from hook start with 13 hdc

Crochet 2 more rows of 13 hdc

In the next 5 rows we decrease every row the last 2 stitches (the last row should have a stitch count of 4 stitches)

Crochet a border of approx. 45 hdc around the whole work

!!! To the top corners crochet in each corner 2x 2 hdc (the same as at the collar) !!!

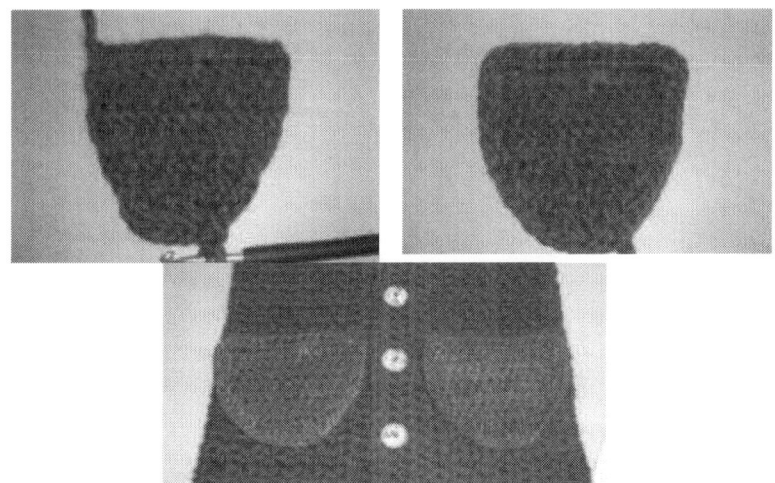

I hope you have fun while working after this pattern

Crochet Pattern Jacket with Pattern

You need
Hook size 7,00 and 6,00mm US J and K UK 4 and 2
Sewing needle, scissor, Buttons

Maxi Merino (100 g = 125 Meter - Chunky)
→ Depending on size 250- 600 Gramm
Yarn "Wolke Hegenbarth" (NS 8,0- 10,0 ---- 50g = 60 Meter - Chunky)
→ 1 Ball
You can of course use every similar yarn.

Preamble

I did think a lot how do I get all the sizes onto paper that you can understand. I hope you are happy with the solution. If you have still some questions feel free to contact me @ kelly@micromarco.de

We start from bottom to top. If not different mentioned start each row with 1 CH.
Waist and Bust
Shoulder Parts
Sleeves
Button Line
Collar or Hoodie

The Pattern

The pattern will be used everywhere except the sleeves.
It is done in 2 Parts Part A and Part B.

Part A
Now you have a chain of the length you need
Crochet 1-2 rows of SC
Now crochet 3 CH
Skip the next stitch and crochet 3 DC in the next 3 stitches
The 4th DC you crochet into the skipped stitch

Part B
One round of SC

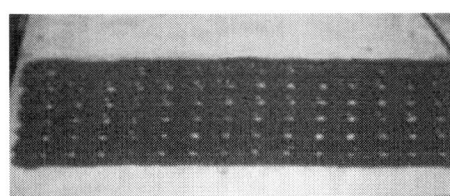

In this table you see the size and the fitting count of CH that you need to cast on (must be a multiple of 4 + 1 +1)

Size 50- 56	→ 42 SC
Size 62- 68	→ 46 SC
Size 74- 80	→ 54 SC
Size 86- 92	→ 62 SC
Size 98- 104	→ 66 SC
Size 110- 116	→ 70 SC
Size 122- 128	→ 78 SC

Now we crochet the before explained pattern.

Part A

You have the chain in the length you need
Now crochet 1-2 row of SC
Now crochet 3 CH
Skip 1 stitch, crochet 3 DC into the next 3 stitches
The 4th DC you crochet into the skipped stitch (see pictures)

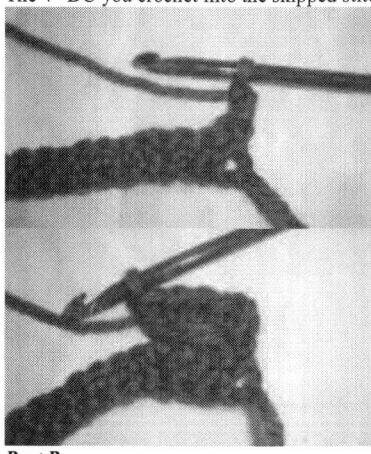

Part B

One round of SC
Now you crochet as many rows as you need. Start every row with 3 CH and skip 1 stitch and so on.
How many rows you need will be shown in the table below.

Size 50- 56

→ 4 rows in the pattern (10 stitch groups in each row) Row 4 till end of part A
→ Part B of row 4: inc every 10th stitch (4 inc = 1 stitch group added)
→ crochet 2 more rows (11 stitch groups in each row). For the last 2 stitches of the row crochet as normal

Size 62- 68

→ 5 rows in pattern (11 stich groups in each row) Row 5 just till end of part A
→ Part B of row 5: inc every 11th stitch (4 inc = 1 stitch group added)
→ crochet 2 more rows (12 stitch groups in each row) For the last 2 stitches of the row just crochet each 1 SC

Size 74- 80

→ 5 rows in pattern (13 stich groups in each row) Row 5 just till end of part A
→ Part B of row 5: inc every 13th stitch (4 inc = 1 stitch group added)
→ crochet 2 more rows (14 stitch groups in each row) For the last 2 stitches of the row just crochet each 1 SC

Size 86- 92
→ 6 rows in pattern (15 stitch groups in each row) Row 6 just till end of part A
→ Part B of row 6: inc every 15th stitch (4 inc = 1 stitch group added)
→ crochet 4 more rows (16 stitch groups in each row) For the last 2 stitches of the row just crochet each 1 SC

Size 98- 104
→ 8 rows in pattern (16 stich groups in each row) Row 8 just till end of part A
→ Part B of row 8: inc every 16th stitch (4 inc = 1 stitch group added)
→ crochet 6 more rows (17 stitch groups in each row) For the last 2 stitches of the row just crochet each 1 SC

Size 110- 116
→ 9 rows in pattern (17 stich groups in each row) Row 9 just till end of part A
→ Part B of row 9: inc every 17th stitch (4 inc = 1 stitch group added)
→ crochet 7 more rows (18 stitch groups in each row) For the last 2 stitches of the row just crochet each 1 SC

Size 122- 128
→ 11 rows in pattern (18 stich groups in each row) Row 11 just till end of part A
→ Part B of row 11: inc every 19th stitch (4 inc = 1 stitch group added)
→ crochet 9 more rows (19 stitch groups in each row) For the last 2 stitches of the row just crochet each 1 SC

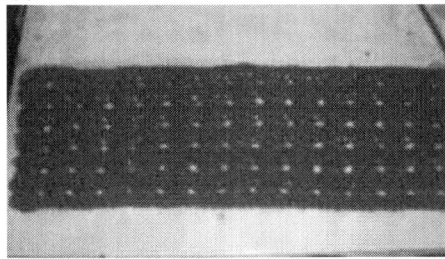

Now we work the shoulders. Take your measurements out of the table below.

At the left side of the work you start at the end of stitch group 3.
→ crochet 3 CH (counts as 1st DC)
→ then another 2 DC
→ now crochet the 4th DC to the right of the 3 CH
→ another stitch group next to it (depending on the size table below)
→ after the last stitch group skip 1 stitch and crochet 1 DC next to it
At the right side of the work you skip the 1st stitch group and crochet as usual:
→ 3 CH
→ skip 1 stitch
→ 3 DC
→ 4th DC into the skipped stitch
→ crochet your amount of stitch groups and rows

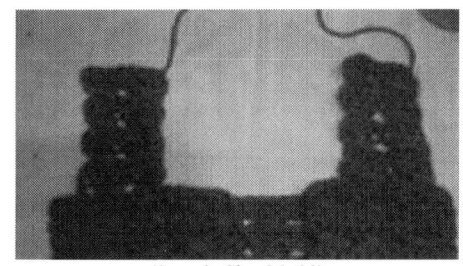

	(Sample Size 86- 92)
Size 50- 56	Width- 2 stitch groups
	Height - 3 Rows
Size 62- 68	Width - 2 stitch groups
	Height - 3 Rows
Size 74- 80	Width - 2 stitch groups
	Height - 4 Rows
Size 86- 92	Width - 2 stitch groups
	Height - 4 Rows
Size 98- 104	Width - 3 stitch groups
	Height - 5 Rows
Size 110- 116	Width - 3 stitch groups
	Height - 6 Rows
Size 122- 128	Width - 4 stitch groups
	Height - 7 Rows

Now we are at the back / neck part

You skip 1 stitch group at the right shoulder part and cast on there the yarn.

→ 3 CH (counts as 1st DC)

→ 2 DC

→ 4 DC to the right of the 3 CH

→ skip 1 stitch and crochet 1 additional DC

→ more stitch group as of the size table

At the end you skip again 1 stitch group to the shoulder part.

Size 50- 56	Width- 3 stitch groups
	Height- 3 Rows
Size 62- 68	Width - 5 stitch groups
	Height - 3 Rows
Size 74- 80	Width - 6 stitch groups
	Height - 4 Rows
Size 86- 92	Width - 8 stitch groups
	Height - 4 Rows
Size 98- 104	Width - 7 stitch groups
	Height - 5 Rows
Size 110- 116	Width - 8 stitch groups
	Height - 6 Rows
Size 122- 128	Width - 7 stitch groups
	Height - 7 Rows

Sew the shoulder and back part at the top together.

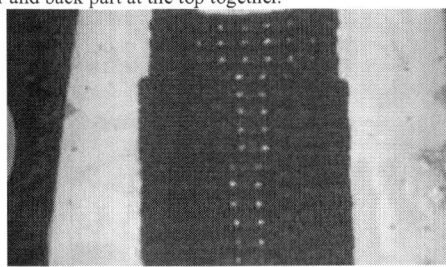

Now we crochet the sleeves

Spread the stitch count (as of size table) to the sleeve hole and crochet 1 round of SC.
The sleeves are made in Part A only. Don't crochet Part B.

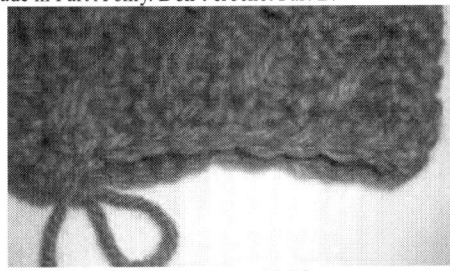

Size 50- 56	28 SC
Size 62- 68	28 SC
Size 74- 80	32 SC
Size 86- 92	32 SC
Size 98- 104	36 SC
Size 110- 116	36 SC
Size 122- 128	40 SC

Now you start with the pattern (without Part B)

→ 3 CH
→ skip 1 stitch
→ 3 DC
→ 4th DC into the skipped stitch
The end of the round looks like:
→ you have 3 skipped stitches

→ skip 1 stitch and crochet 2 DC; the 1st DC (3 CH) from the start of the round will be part of the stitch group
→ connect now the 2 parts with 1 slst
→ crochet now the 4th DC into the skipped stitch

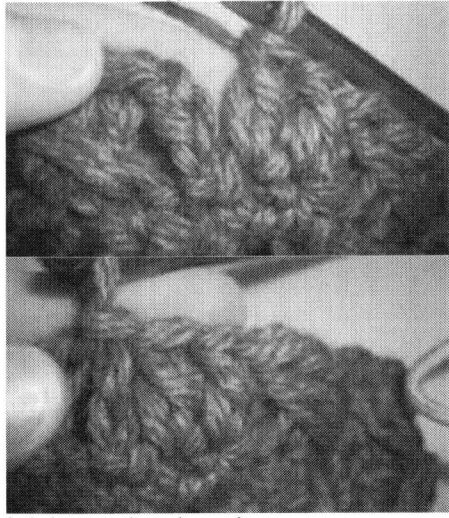

This is the count of stitch groups in each round:

Size 50- 56   7 stitch groups
Size 62- 68   7 stitch groups
Size 74- 80   8 stitch groups
Size 86- 92   8 stitch groups
Size 98- 104   9 stitch groups
Size 110- 116   9 stitch groups
Size 122- 128   10 stitch groups

And this is the count of rounds you need to crochet:

Size 50- 56   6 Rounds with hook size 7,00mm then 3 rounds with hook size 6,00mm
Size 62- 68   7 Rounds with hook size 7,00mm then 3 rounds with hook size 6,00mm
Size 74- 80   8 Rounds with hook size 7,00mm then 3 rounds with hook size 6,00mm
Size 86- 92   9 Rounds with hook size 7,00mm then 3 rounds with hook size 6,00mm
Size 98- 104   9 Rounds with hook size 7,00mm then 3 rounds with hook size 6,00mm
Size 110- 116   10 Rounds with hook size 7,00mm then 3 rounds with hook size 6,00mm
Size 122- 128   10 Rounds with hook size 7,00mm then 3 rounds with hook size 6,00mm

At the end crochet in white 2-4 round of SC. depending on your choice
(Sample Size 86- 92)

The button border

Cast on at the left side of the jacket and spread the SC as below:

Size 50- 56	18 SC	over 4 Rows
Size 62- 68	21 SC	over 5 Rows
Size 74- 80	21 SC	over 6 Rows
Size 86- 92	28 SC	over 7 Rows
Size 98- 104	42 SC	over 8 Rows
Size 110- 116	48 SC	over 9 Rows
Size 122- 128	60 SC	over 10 Rows

At the right side of the jacket spread also the same count of stitches as below.

Size 50- 56	18 SC	over 1 Row
Size 62- 68	21 SC	over 1 Row
Size 74- 80	21 SC	over 2 Rows
Size 86- 92	28 SC	over 3 Rows
Size 98- 104	42 SC	over 4 Rows
Size 110- 116	48 SC	over 5 Rows
Size 122- 128	60 SC	over 6 Rows

Now we crochet the button holes. Now it gets a little tricky. First think about how many
buttons you like to have and what size they should have. Place a marker at this places
where the buttons should be.
You start (depending on the button size) to crochet CH on the place where the button will
be, skip 1-3 stitches and crochet SC till the next button hole.

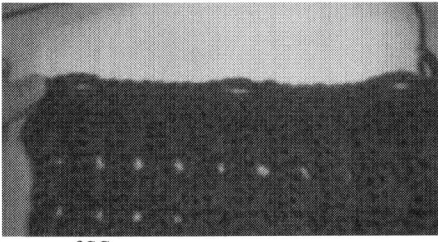

Now crochet another row of SC.
1 SC in each stitch.
Into the chain bows you crochet as much SC as you have CH
Crochet 1 row of SC again 1 SC in each stitch.

Collar

Now spread over evenly SC. from the left button border over to the right button border.
At the end you should have a stitch count that is a multiple of 4 + 2.
e.g. 24+ 2   so 26 SC in one row
Then you crochet the pattern (Part A and B). the amount of stitch groups are depending on
the amount of spread SC.

The first both parts of B crochet with white.
The amount of rows in each size you will find in the table below:

Size 50- 56	3 Rows
Size 62- 68	4 Rows
Size 74- 80	5 Rows
Size 86- 92	5 Rows
Size 98- 104	6 Rows
Size 110- 116	7 Rows
Size 122- 128	8 Rows

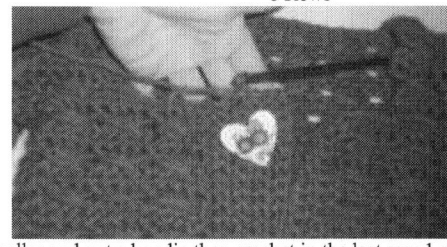

If you just like a collar and not a hoodie then crochet in the last row 1 row of SC and cut the yarn.

Now make a border in white.

Start at the bottom left corner of the button border

→ over the bottom border

→ up the right button border

→ over the collar

→ down the left button border

→ close the border with 1 slst into the 1st white SC

→ 1 CH, cut yarn

Hoodie

Here is the table for the rows for the hoodie:

Size 50- 56	7 Rows
Size 62- 68	8 Rows
Size 74- 80	10 Rows
Size 86- 92	10 Rows
Size 98- 104	11 Rows
Size 110- 116	12 Rows
Size 122- 128	13 Rows

Now make a border around the jacket in white.

Start at the bottom left button border

→ around the bottom border

→ up the right button border

→ around the collar

→ down the left button border

→ close the border with 1 slst into the 1st white SC

→ 1 CH, cut the yarn

Done is the jacket. :)

Printed in Great Britain
by Amazon